WE BOTH READ®

Parent's Introduction

We Both Read is the first series of books designed to invite parents and children to share the reading of a story by taking turns reading aloud. This "shared reading" innovation, which was developed in conjunction with early reading specialists, invites parents to read the more sophisticated text on the left-hand pages, while children are encouraged to read the right-hand pages, which have been written at one of three early reading levels.

Reading aloud is one of the most important activities parents can share with their child to assist their reading development. However, *We Both Read* goes beyond reading *to* a child and allows parents to share reading *with* a child. *We Both Read* is so powerful and effective because it combines two key elements in learning: "showing" (the parent reads) and "doing" (the child reads). The result is not only faster reading development for the child, but a much more enjoyable and enriching experience for both!

Most of the words used in the child's text should be familiar to them. Others can easily be sounded out. An occasional difficult word will be first introduced in the parent's text, distinguished with **bold lettering**. Pointing out these words, as you read them, will help familiarize them to your child. You may also find it helpful to read the entire book aloud yourself the first time, then invite your child to participate on the second reading. Also note that the parent's text is preceded by a "talking parent" icon: ☺ ; and the child's text is preceded by a "talking child" icon: ☺ .

We Both Read books is a fun, easy way to encourage and help your child to read — and a wonderful way to start your child off on a lifetime of reading enjoyment!

We Both Read: About the Ocean

———————————————

Use of photographs provided by PhotoDisc (Digital Imagery © copyright 2001 PhotoDisc., Inc.).
Use of other images provided by Corbis Images.

We Both Read® is a registered trademark of Treasure Bay, Inc.

Published by Treasure Bay, Inc.
40 Sir Francis Drake Blvd.
San Anselmo, CA 94960 USA

PRINTED IN SINGAPORE

Library of Congress Catalog Card Number: 2001 131568

Hardcover ISBN: 1-891327-31-3
Paperback ISBN: 1-891327-32-1

05 06 07 08 09 / 10 9 8 7 6 5 4 3

We Both Read® Books
Patent No. 5,957,693

Visit us online at:
www.webothread.com

WE BOTH READ®

About the Ocean

By Sindy McKay

TREASURE BAY

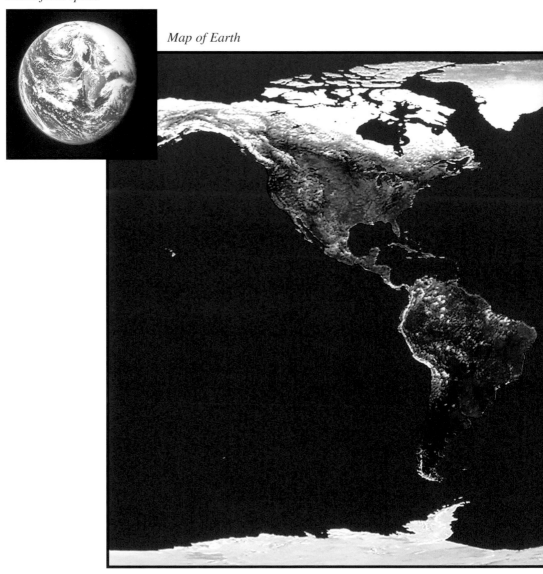

Earth from space

Map of Earth

Imagine you are a space alien flying high above the earth. You look down at the beautiful planet below and what do you see?

Water! You see lots and lots of water. And most of that water is contained in the **oceans** of **earth**.

👀 The **earth** is covered by much more water than land. You could fit all the land on the earth into the **oceans** three times!

 There are four major oceans on earth. They are the **Pacific,** the Atlantic, the Indian, and the Arctic. There are also many smaller seas.

These oceans and most seas are all really one large connected body of water broken up by big pieces of land we call continents.

The **Pacific** is the biggest ocean. You can sail
on it for many days and never see land.

Reef in Red Sea

Humpback whale

ᴄᴏ   When we look out at the ocean we see a vast expanse of
water. But when we look under the ocean's surface, we find
an amazing world filled with deep trenches, high mountains,
dark caves and colorful coral reefs. We also find an enormous
variety of plants and **animals** from the tiny krill to the mighty
whale.

 There are very small **animals** in the ocean.
They are so small you can't even see them.
There are very big animals. **Whales** are some
of the biggest animals to ever live on earth!

Little boys playing in a tide pool

Life in the ocean can be divided into three major groups. The first group, called the plankton, includes the plants and animals that **move** and drift with the currents and tides.

Many of these life forms can be found in tide pools, but most are so tiny you need a **strong** microscope to see them.

These kinds of animals are not very **strong.**
The water pushes them around. That is mainly
how they **move** from one place to the next.

Sea squirt

Another group of plants and animals, called the benthos, live on or in the ocean floor. They can be found throughout the ocean, from the shore to the greatest depths of the **sea.**

This group contains such unique life forms as coral, sponges, anemones, **sea** star, crabs, clams, and sea squirts.

 Some people call this animal a starfish. But it is not a fish at all. The real name for it is a **sea star**.

The giant clam seen in this **picture** has a body made up of two shells connected by large, strong muscles. That's why it's so hard to open a clamshell!

This is a sea fan. It looks like a plant, but it is an animal. There is another animal in this **picture,** too. Can you find him?

Red hogfish

The third major group of plants and animals in the ocean is called the nekton. These creatures swim freely through the water and include some of the most familiar of all sea life.

A few of the creatures that belong in this group are whales, **sharks,** manta rays, sea turtles, and well over 20,000 **different** species of fish.

Whale shark and scuba divers

There are many **different** kinds of **shark.** The biggest is called the whale shark. It is the biggest fish in the ocean.

School of anthias fish

Some kinds of fish swim together in large groups called **schools.** Schools are usually made up of fish that are eaten by larger predatory fish. Maybe there really is safety in numbers!

Zebra lionfish

Not all fish swim in **schools.** This fish is the kind that likes to eat other fish.

Killer whale

Most of the animals in the ocean are able to breathe underwater. But some ocean animals need to come to the surface to breathe.

Whales and **dolphins** are mammals, just like us, and they would drown if they could not get to the surface for air.

 Dolphins love to play. People like to watch them swim and jump.

Sea **turtles** spend most of their time in the water, only coming to the surface to breathe. The only time they actually leave the ocean is to lay **their** eggs under the sand on the beach. About two months later, the baby turtles are born.

Baby sea **turtles** are born under the sand. They have to dig **their** way out. Then they have to find their way to the ocean.

There are many animals that don't live under the ocean, but still depend on it to live. These include sea birds and marine mammals that live on or near the ocean's shore.

Sea birds come in many different shapes and sizes. One of the most unusual birds is the **penguin.**

 **Penguins** do not fly in the sky like most birds. They use their wings to help them swim. Some people say that they fly under the water!

Sea lions, walruses, sea **otters,** and seals are mammals that spend much of their lives in the ocean. They might move slowly and clumsily on land, but they are swift and graceful in the water.

 Most sea **otters** sleep on their backs in the water.

All sea otters eat on their backs in the water.

People also depend on the ocean. Since early times, humans have chosen to build cities near the water so they could harvest its endless bounty.

People use the ocean in many ways. They get food from it. They use it to get from place to place. They even use it to have fun!

When most people think of the food that comes from the ocean they think of fish. But there are many other kinds of food we harvest from the sea. In some countries, **seaweed** is used to make all kinds of delicious dishes!

Do you eat ice cream? Then you may have eaten **seaweed.** One kind of seaweed is often used to make ice cream thick.

Moving people and things across the vast ocean can be a real challenge. So humans have built ships and boats of every size, from huge **freighters** to sleek sailboats to fancy cruise ships.

🐣 **Freighters** are big ships that move things from one place to another place. They can carry cars, food, toys, and even airplanes.

Long ago big sailing ships would set out to **cruise** across the ocean. Occasionally one would end up sinking to the bottom of the sea.

These old sunken ships are sometimes thought to be filled with treasure. Do you think this one has any treasures on board?

Cruise ships carry people across the ocean today. Most people who take these ships love the sea. And they love to have fun!

Surfer surfing a big wave

There are many ways to have fun in and on the ocean. You can swim, surf, sail, snorkel, collect **seashells,** and so much more!

Young girl listening to a seashell

 **Seashells** come in many sizes. Some are very small and some are very large.

Some people think you can hear the ocean inside a seashell.

Snorkeling is a great way to see what's going on underwater. It's wonderful to discover such an amazing world lying just beneath the ocean's surface.

Grandfather and grandson fishing

Many people fish to get food. But some people do it just because they like to. It's a nice way to spend time with friends and family.

 Unfortunately, one other way that humans use the ocean is as a dumping ground. Everything from trash to sewage to toxic waste goes into the sea.

We used to think that the ocean could handle all that pollution, but now we know it can't.

You can help. You can find out more about the ocean. You can share all you know with other people.

Coral reef

The more you know about the ocean, the more you appreciate how important it is. It is one of our most precious resources. Life on earth could not exist without it.

If we help take care of the ocean, the ocean will help take care of us.

If you liked
About The Ocean, here are two other
We Both Read® Books you are sure to enjoy!

Over 20 different kinds of insects are featured in
this non-fiction book in the *We Both Read*™ series.
With 40 pages of amazing photographs of the insect
world, this book relates fascinating facts about these
six-legged creatures that will enthrall children and
parents alike!